Our New Neighbors

by

Barbara Herkimer

AuthorHouse™
1663 Liberty Drive
Bloomington, IN 47403
www.authorhouse.com
Phone: 1-800-839-8640

First published by AuthorHouse 7/27/2009

ISBN: 978-1-4490-0615-0 (sc)

Library of Congress Control Number: 2009907284

Printed in the United States of America
Bloomington, Indiana

This book is printed on acid-free paper.

authorHOUSE®

Our new neighbors came to call.

They are black and fuzzy from their heads to their toes, and their eyes are tiny, but their noses are big. And that is so they can smell their next meal, which might be as far as three miles away.

**Mama bear has
twin bear cubs,**

as you can see, and she must
keep them safe from you
and me.

Mama and her baby bear cubs eat grass, nuts, roots, and berries.

They will turn over old woodpiles to find nice and tasty bugs, too.

Mama knows best for the twin bear cubs.

She will watch her babies ever so carefully, and if there is any
danger nearby, up the tree they will climb,

**where they
will wait…**

and wait...

...until
Mama says
everything is
safe;

only then will they
come down to play.

The bear cubs had fun
when they came to call.

They played in our hammock all day long.

Oh, how they really listened to their Mama.

And if they forgot to be good, she would snort from her big bear nose to remind them to behave. After a while, Mama and her babies became tired and went to take a nap during the hottest part of the day. But one little baby kept his eyes open and his nose up in the air, sniffing around. Mama pulled them both closer with her big bear paw to help settle them down for their nap.

Many days passed as we people watched our new neighbors grow, getting bigger and stronger.

Mama bear taught them what bears do. But every now and then they would forget to listen.

It happened one day when our chickens were running around outside...

One of the bear cubs started chasing a chicken, and she started squawking and running away, flapping her wings as fast as she could.

Mama bear stopped that young bear cub by swinging her big paw in the air while walking toward her cub and snorting.

Baby bear stopped to listen. Holding his head down low, he walked slowly back to Mama.

Later they followed Mama toward some nice, ripe blueberries that were all good enough to eat.

They all seemed to enjoy the berries very much...

We have two cats, one an older and wiser black and white cat whose name is Coby, and the other a young, dark tiger kitten whose name is Emma.

Well, one day Emma thought she was a brave wildcat and crept up ever so slowly to the bears, who were over near the trees.

Coby, being older and wiser, meowed to warn Emma, but she did not listen and crept closer, making her way to the bushes near Mama Bear.

Well, Mama Bear saw Emma and stomped her front paws down to the ground while snorting a big bear snort.

Emma ran out of the bushes and back to the house as fast as she could run. Coby knew best that day, and Emma learned to watch the bears from far away.

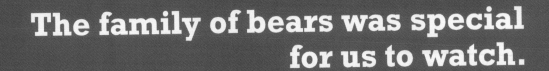

The family of bears was special for us to watch.

Mama Bear loved her babies as all Mamas do, and she would protect them as best as she knew.

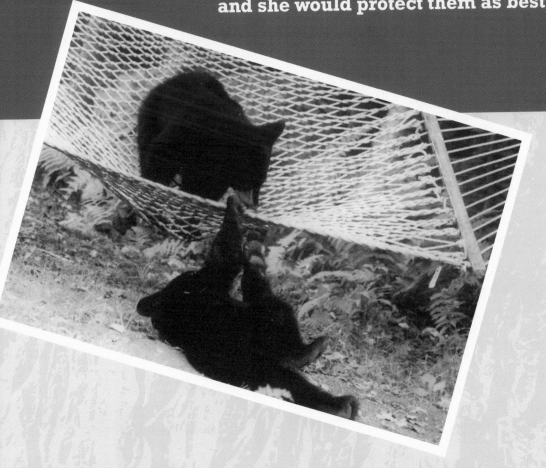

As spring became summer and summer turned into fall, we watched the young family grow bigger and fatter, as bears should when the cold wind begins to blow.

Mama and her cubs grew a nice, thick layer of softer, warmer fur under their summer coats to keep them very warm for the winter months.

And Mama found a nice place for them to snuggle up together and hibernate.

Mama gave them both a big bear hug, and they all snuggled down together for their long winter nap.

LaVergne, TN USA
12 November 2009
163557LV00003B